All About Your

Senses

Donna Bailey

STECK-VAUGHN
LIBRARY
A Division of Steck-Vaughn Company

Austin, Texas

How to Use This Book

This book tells you many things about your five senses. There is a Table of Contents on the next page. It shows you what each double page of the book is about. For example, pages 10 and 11 tell you about "Senses and the Brain."

On many of these pages you will find words that are printed in **bold** type. The bold type shows you that these words are in the Glossary on pages 46 and 47. The Glossary explains the meaning of some words that may be new to you.

At the very end of the book there is an Index. The Index tells you where to find certain words in the book. For example, you can use it to look up words like epidermis, sensory receptors, papillae, and many other words to do with your five senses.

Printed and bound in the United States
1 2 3 4 5 6 7 8 9 0 LB 95 94 93 92 91

Library of Congress Cataloging-in-Publication Data

Bailey, Donna.
    All about your senses / Donna Bailey.
      p. cm.—(Health facts)
    Rev. ed. of: The five senses / Jacqueline Dineen. 1988.
    Includes index.
    Summary: Discusses the functions, disorders, and care of the five senses.
    ISBN 0-8114-2776-5
    1. Senses and sensation—Juvenile literature.
[1. Senses and sensation.] I. Dineen, Jacqueline. Five senses. II. Title. III. Series: Bailey, Donna. Health facts.
QP434.B35 1990   90-10051
612.8—dc20   CIPAC

Contents

Introduction

Your five **senses** are your senses of touch, taste, smell, hearing, and sight. Your senses tell you what is going on all around you.

The tennis player in the picture is concentrating and using all his senses. His eyes and ears are passing messages to and from his **brain** along a network of **nerves.**

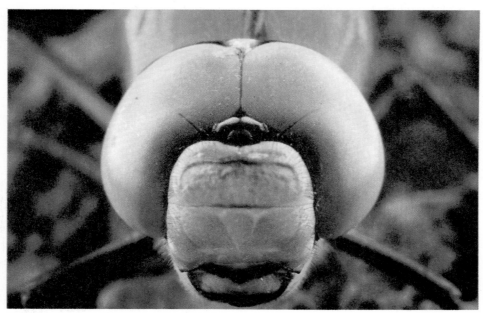

the round eyes of a dragonfly

Animals' senses are not all the same.
A dog's sense of smell is about 100
times better than a human being's.
The dog in the picture can find
someone buried in snow by smelling them.

A dragonfly has very good eyes.
Humans only have one **lens** in each
eye, but a dragonfly has up to 30,000
lenses in each of its big round eyes.
These help it find insects for food.

Finding Out

Thousands of years ago, people used to hunt animals for their food, like the hunter in the picture does today. Hunters need good senses to see animals and hear them moving.

The first hunters did not know how any of their five senses worked. Hippocrates, who lived in Greece over 2,000 years ago, was the first person to link the brain with the senses.

About 700 years ago, doctors were only just beginning to understand how our senses work.

The picture shows an eye doctor giving a patient glasses 400 years ago.

The first ear trumpets were made 300 years ago to help people who could not hear well. An ear trumpet made sounds louder and easier to hear.

using an ear trumpet

A Network of Nerves

Sensory nerves carry signals to and from our senses to the spinal cord. These signals travel up the spinal cord to the brain which sends messages back along the same way.

Each sensory nerve has a tiny nerve ending called a **sensory receptor.** The picture, taken under a **microscope,** shows a sensory receptor in the skin.

the spinal cord links the brain and the sensory nerves

nerves

spinal cord

brain

spinal cord

bones protecting spinal cord

nerves

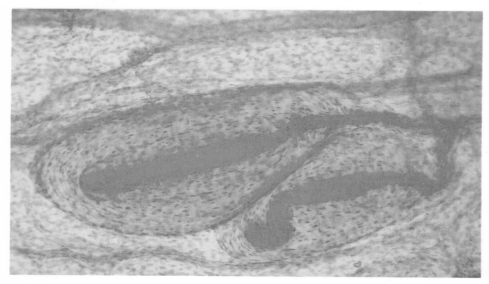

sensory receptors in the skin

Each sensory receptor picks up a feeling and sends a tiny electric current along the nerves and spinal cord to the brain. The brain takes in the information and tells the **motor nerves** what to do.

The racing driver in the picture is escaping from his burning car. His eyes see the flames, his nose smells the smoke, and his skin feels the heat. His brain sends messages to his motor nerves to make his **muscles** work fast.

Senses and the Brain

Different parts of the brain control different actions, such as speaking, or the movement of your limbs.

The smaller, back part of the brain is called the **cerebellum.** This controls your balance and the way your muscles work together.

The brain receives the messages from all over the body and decides what to do. Different parts of the brain control different actions, such as speech and movement of the limbs. Messages are sent out from these areas.

touch

cerebellum

B

smell

D

C

A

hearing

sight

spinal cord

cerebrum

section A deals with sight

section B deals with the sense of touch

Section C controls hearing

The largest part of the brain is the **cerebrum** which controls all **voluntary** movements as well as thought and memory. The cerebrum is covered by a wrinkled layer of **cortex** where most of the brain's work is done.

Different parts of the brain control your touch, smell, hearing, and sight.

Section D controls smell

Skin and Touch

Your skin is made up of layers of tiny **cells,** packed closely together. The top layer is the **epidermis.** The **dermis** underneath it has millions of sensory receptors which sense pain, pressure, heat and cold, and touch. Touch receptors can tell whether an object is smooth or rough.

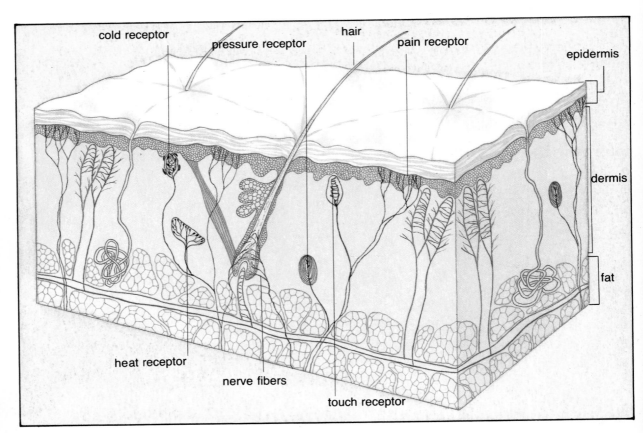

cold receptor
pressure receptor
hair
pain receptor
epidermis
dermis
fat
heat receptor
nerve fibers
touch receptor

your tongue does not feel heat and cold well, so a hot drink may scald it

Pressure receptors tell the brain if something is pressing on you too hard.

The most important receptors are the pain receptors, which are found all over the body. They warn the brain that something is harming you.

There are more touch receptors in your tongue, lips, fingertips, and hair roots than in the other parts of your body. The middle of your back has the fewest receptors.

cold receptors in the skin make goose pimples to help keep you warm

Using Touch

Your sense of touch is very important for **communication.**
It helps you let other people know how you feel about them.
When you meet someone and shake hands, this is more friendly than just saying, "hello."

The mother in the picture is giving her son a hug as she reads to him.
This shows him how much she loves him.

Some people use their sense of touch in their work. The tailor in this picture uses his sense of touch to help choose and cut cloth.

Your skin helps you cool down if you get too hot. **Pores** in your skin open. **Sweat** runs out, **evaporates,** and makes your skin cooler.

drops of sweat on the skin cool you down

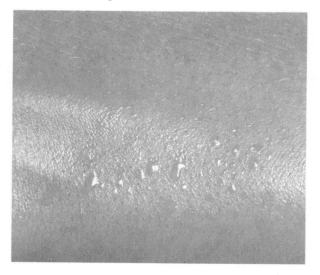

Tasting Food

If you look at your tongue in a
mirror, you can see bumps called
papillae all over the top of it.
Each papilla has 100–200 **taste buds.**
The picture, taken under a microscope,
shows a single taste bud.

Each taste bud has receptor cells
arranged in groups, making a hollow.
Every receptor cell has tiny taste
hairs on the end which pick up the
taste of the food.

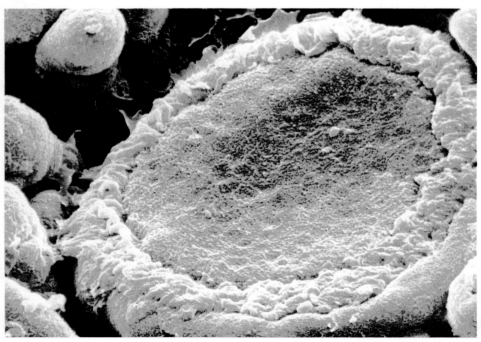

**how we taste
things**

Try putting small amounts of something sweet, salty, sour, and bitter on your tongue in turn. Can you tell which parts of your tongue are sensitive to the different tastes?

bitterness

A Taste Bud

nerve fibers

sensory cell

saltiness

sweetness

sourness

The taste buds at the back of your tongue taste anything bitter, and you taste sour things along the sides of the tongue. You taste salty things in the center, and sweet things at the front of the tongue.

you taste ice cream at the front of the tongue

A Sense of Smell

When you breathe, you draw air up through your nose into a large space behind the nose called the **nasal cavity.** At the top of the nasal cavity are sensory receptors with tiny hairs which pick up smells from the air. The nerves at the end of the receptor cells then send a signal to the brain.

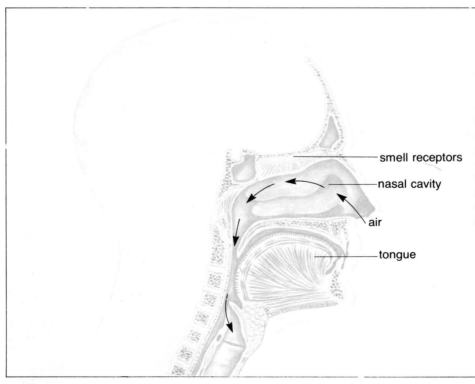

smell receptors

nasal cavity

air

tongue

The area of the nasal cavity is only 1 sq. in., but it contains 5 million receptors. These lead to 15,000 nerve fibers which carry information about smell to the brain. Each receptor responds to one type of smell only. The receptors combine to identify the thousands of different smells around us.

Your sense of taste is linked to your sense of smell.

If you shut your eyes and hold your nose when you are eating, you will find it difficult to taste the food. When you have a bad cold and a blocked nose you cannot taste anything.

**you can tell by the smell
if milk is fresh or sour**

How We Hear

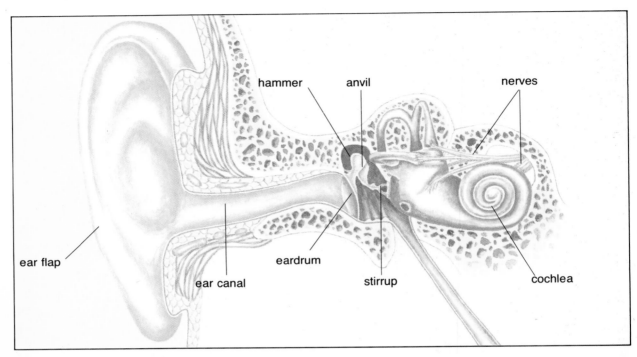

Your ear flap traps sounds and sends
them down the ear canal to the
eardrum. The sound waves strike the
eardrum and make it **vibrate.** Three
tiny bones behind the eardrum, the
hammer, the stirrup, and the anvil
pick up the vibrations and pass them
to the **cochlea** in the inner ear. Cells
in the cochlea change these
vibrations into nerve signals.

**stop, look, and listen
before you cross the street**

Animals hear more sounds than humans. Some whistles have a high pitched note a dog can hear but a human cannot.

when we talk to each other, we often use our hands to help explain what we mean

Ears and Balance

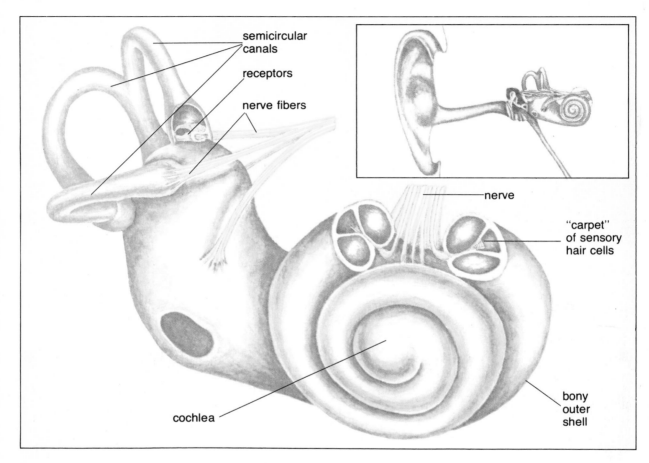

semicircular canals

receptors

nerve fibers

nerve

"carpet" of sensory hair cells

bony outer shell

cochlea

You use your ears to help you balance.
Three **semicircular canals** in the
inner ear are filled with the same
liquid that is inside the cochlea.
When you move, the liquid moves, and
tiny hairs inside the semicircular
canals send signals to the brain.

whirling round and round can make you dizzy

When you are spun around on a carnival ride, the liquid inside the semi-circular canals swirls around inside your ears. This makes the hairs of the sensory cells bend in all directions. The signals from the sensory cells confuse the brain. This makes you feel dizzy.

a tightrope walker has a very good sense of balance

Hearing Problems

Very loud noise can damage your ears. Some people today have poor hearing from listening to very loud music at clubs or rock concerts.

Doctors can test your hearing.
The boy in the picture is wearing
headphones so that he can only hear
sounds coming from the machine.
He tells the doctor which sounds he
can hear well and the doctor marks
them down.

You must take care of your ears
and keep them clean. If dust and dirt
get inside the ear they can damage
the eardrum. Never try to push
anything into your ears, as this can
damage them.

Coping with Deafness

A baby learns to speak by listening
to sounds and trying to copy them.
Deaf children cannot hear sounds and
may have difficulty learning to speak.

Speech therapists can use special
electronic equipment to help some
children with speech problems.
The girl in the picture is watching
the screen as she speaks to see when
she is making the right sounds.

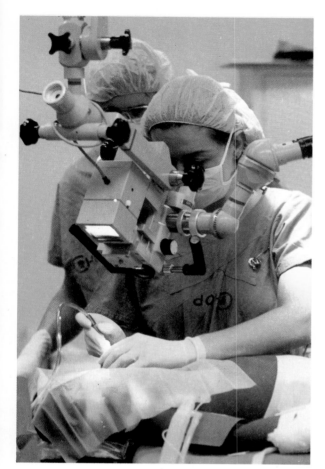

**an ear surgeon operates
on a child's ear**

Some hearing problems can be solved by an operation on the ear.

Deaf children are often taught to speak and "hear" by learning to **lip-read.** Teachers show the child how to recognize the shape the mouth makes in forming different words.

Other kinds of deafness can be helped by wearing a **hearing aid.**

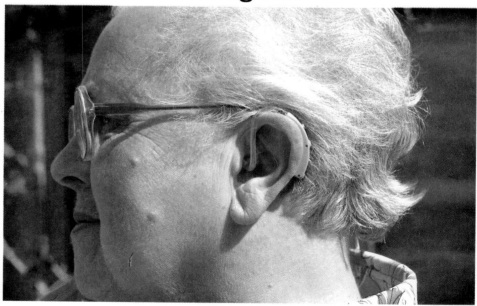

**wearing a
hearing aid**

How the Eye Works

The colored part of your eye, the **iris,** and the black hole in the middle, the **pupil,** are protected by a clear layer called the **cornea.** Behind the pupil is the lens.

Light enters the eye through the cornea, the pupil, and the lens. The image is shown upside-down on the **retina** at the back of the eye.

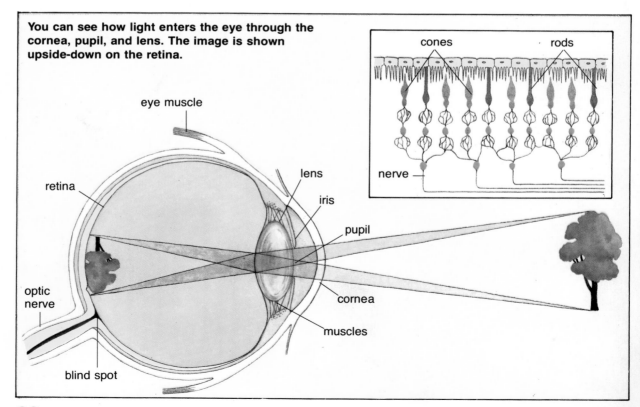

You can see how light enters the eye through the cornea, pupil, and lens. The image is shown upside-down on the retina.

cones   rods

nerve

eye muscle

lens

iris

pupil

retina

cornea

optic nerve

muscles

blind spot

The retina has millions of tiny receptor cells called **cones,** which tell us about the colors we see.
Rods tell us about black and white things we see. The receptor cells send messages to the nerves along the **optic nerve.**

Where the nerves leave the eye there is a **blind spot** on the retina where there are no rods or cones.

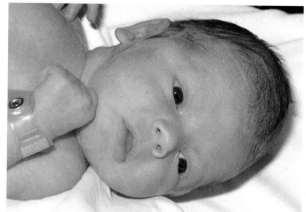

a newborn baby cannot focus like an older child

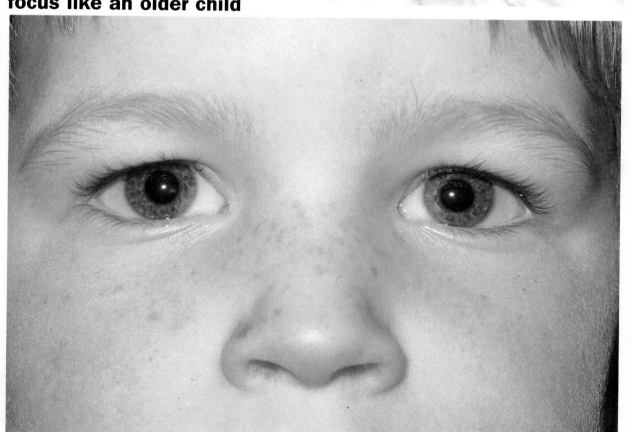

Eye Tests

When light enters the eye, the lens bends the light to **focus** it on the retina. **Nearsighted** people have long eyeballs, so they need to wear glasses with **concave** lenses to help them focus the light on the retina. **Farsighted** people have short eyeballs, so they wear glasses with **convex** lenses to help their eyes to focus.

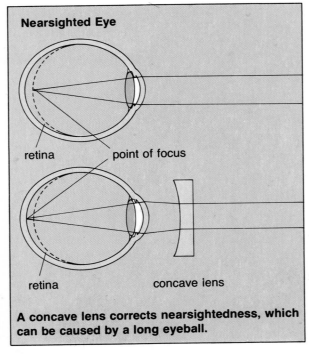

Nearsighted Eye

retina

point of focus

retina

concave lens

A concave lens corrects nearsightedness, which can be caused by a long eyeball.

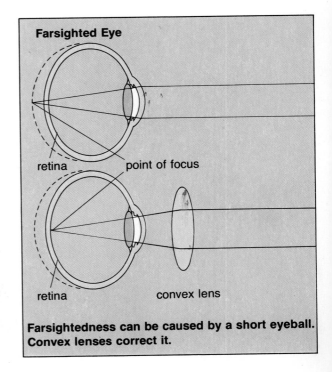

Farsighted Eye

retina

point of focus

retina

convex lens

Farsightedness can be caused by a short eyeball. Convex lenses correct it.

can you see the hidden number in this test for color blindness?

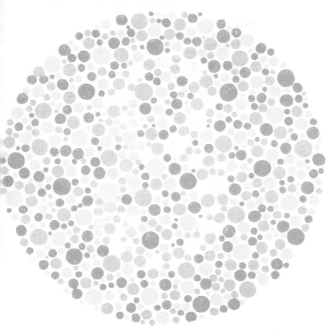

Some people are **color blind** and cannot tell the difference between certain colors because the cones on the retina are faulty.

Sometimes poor sight can develop without you realizing it. When your eyes are tested and you find it difficult to see any of the letters, you may need to wear glasses for some things such as reading.

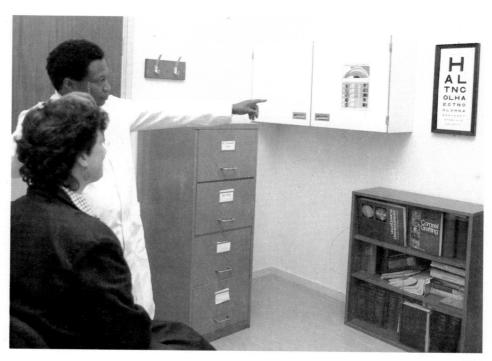

an eye test

Problems with the Eyes

Illness can often affect how your eyes look. If you are fit and healthy, the white part of the eye or **sclera** looks clear.

Sometimes you can see tiny red threads running through the sclera. This is a sign of tiredness or poor health.

The person in the photograph has an eye infection which makes the sclera look bloodshot.

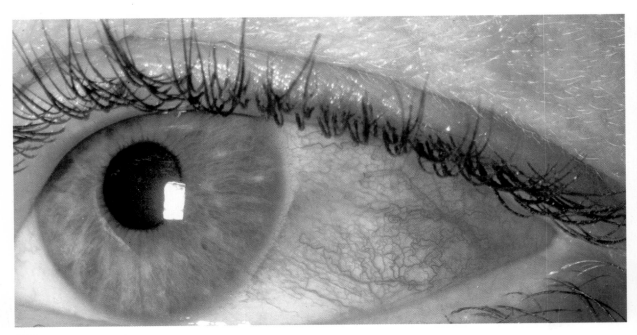

Straw, dust, and pollen can cause **hay fever,** which can make your eyes water and get red and itchy.

When your eyes water or you have tears in the eyes, this helps wash away any dust and dirt that may damage the eyes.
If onion fumes make you cry, your tears wash away the fumes and soreness.

Treating the Eyes

If your eyes are sore, you can sometimes soothe them by using eye drops. More serious problems have to be treated in the hospital.

A doctor cannot always tell what is wrong just by looking at the outside of the eyes. Sometimes the doctor uses an **ophthalmoscope** to look right inside the eye and see the different parts.

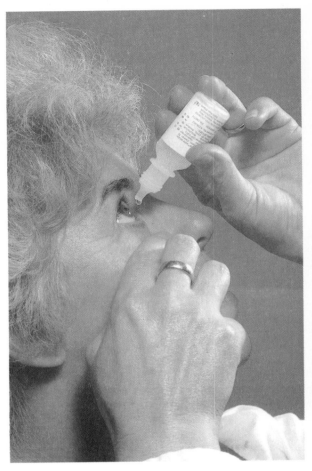

looking inside a patient's eyes

Some eye problems can only be corrected by surgery. Eye surgery is very difficult to do, because our eyes are so small. Before an operation, the surgeon takes a photograph of the inside of the eye, to see what is wrong.

The picture below is a photograph of the inside of an eye, taken through the pupil.

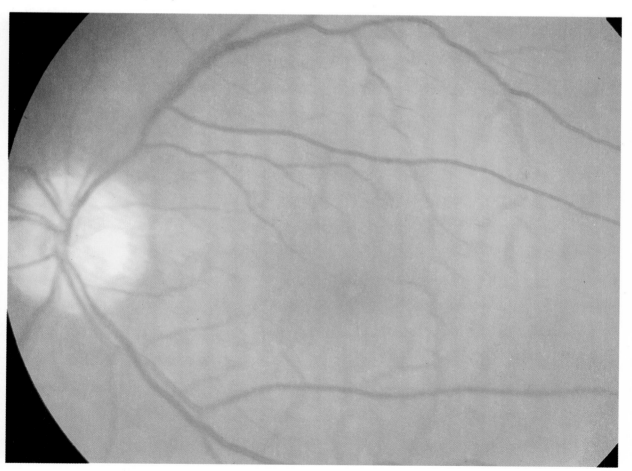

Blindness

Some people are born blind.
They have never seen any of the
things in the world around them.
Others become blind through illness
or an accident.

The first thing blind people must
learn is how to get around safely.
Some blind people use a white cane
to feel their way around. Others
have a guide dog which is trained
to lead its owner along.

**crossing the
street with
the help of
a guide dog**

a children's book in braille

Blind people learn to use their senses of touch, hearing, and smell to replace their sight. They can read books by learning to read **braille.** They feel the dots on the page with their fingers.

Blind people can often learn to do difficult jobs by using special machinery to help them.

using a machine to study

Lost to the World

If you play a game of blind man's bluff, the person who is blindfolded loses all sense of direction.
A loss of any of the senses is called **sensory deprivation** and after a time it can become quite frightening.

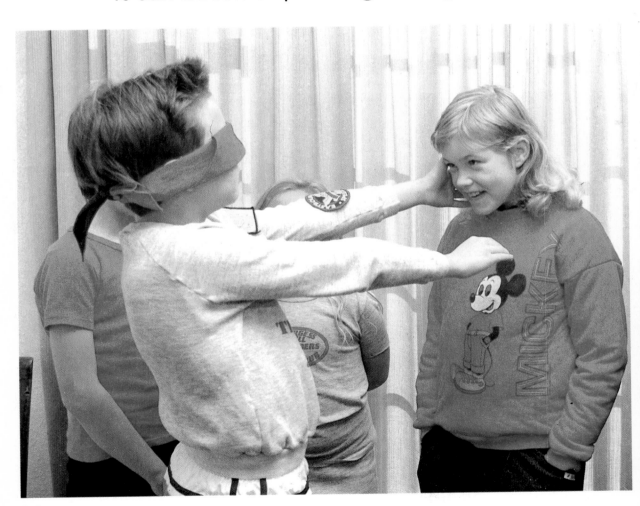

Some people practice to develop their senses. This tea-tasting expert uses his sense of smell and taste to find out the difference between teas.

Other people can learn to control their bodies so that they do not feel pain. Their training helps them to walk on hot coals, or to lie on a bed of nails.

never try walking across burning coals like this man

Safety First

We need our senses to tell us about the world around us, so we must make sure that we take care of them. Workers often wear special clothing. The man in the picture is wearing overalls and gloves to protect his skin, and a helmet to protect his eyes and ears from the noise and dust.

Dark glasses and goggles protect our eyes from dazzling light which can damage them.

Aircraft noise can damage the hearing of people who live near an airport.

Noise levels are measured in **decibels.** A jet aircraft has a level of 130 decibels and a road drill has a noise level of 120 decibels. These levels are dangerous. People who are near these noises for a long time need to wear ear plugs or special earmuffs to protect their ears.

To the Rescue

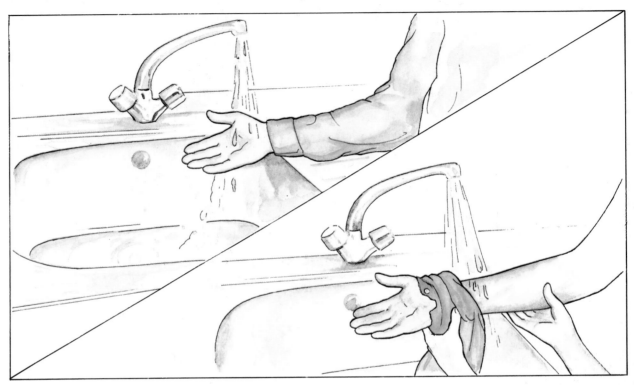

If there is an accident, stay calm
and call an adult right away.
You can sometimes help someone
before help arrives, but you must
know exactly what to do. Groups like
the Red Cross run courses to teach
people first aid.

Large burns, wounds, and other
injuries must be treated by a doctor.

sips of water can help a scalded mouth

If someone has spilled bleach or other household **chemicals** that burn the skin, wash the spot in cold running water for at least ten minutes. Take off any clothing with the chemical still on it.

If someone has scalded their mouth or throat, small sips of water will help to ease the pain.

An insect in the ear can sometimes be washed out with lukewarm water.

never try to dig anything out of the ear

43

Hearing and Seeing

Porpoises, bats, moths, and dogs can hear very high-pitched sounds.

Dolphins have the best sense of hearing of any animals. Their hearing is nearly twice as good as bats, with the next best hearing, and 14 times better than a human's.

Dolphins make very high-pitched sounds, which scientists think help them communicate with each other underwater.

In humans the **auditory** nerve carries messages from 25,000 receptors in the ear to the brain. If this nerve is damaged, it may cause deafness.

There are many inventions to help people who have faulty senses. This robotic dog with electronic "eyes" was made in Japan to act as a guide dog for the blind.

a magnified section of the auditory nerve

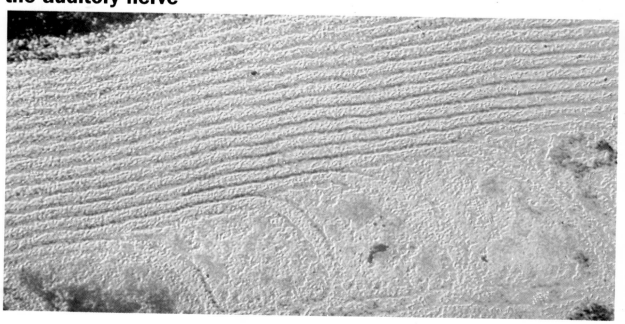

Glossary

auditory to do with hearing.

blind spot the point where the nerve leaves the back of the eye that does not pick up light.

braille a special alphabet for blind people made up of patterns of raised dots. Each pattern stands for a letter of the alphabet.

brain the "computer" in our heads that controls everything we do.

cell a very small part or unit. Most living things are made up of millions of cells.

cerebellum an area at the base of the brain that helps you to stand upright and to move.

cerebrum the largest part of the brain that controls thinking, intelligence, memory, and feelings.

chemical any substance that can change when joined or mixed with another.

cochlea a coiled tube in the inner ear in which sound vibrations are turned into nerve signals.

color blind when someone cannot make out the difference between colors.

communication the exchange of information.

concave curved inward.

cones cells at the back of the eye that see colors.

convex curving outward.

cornea the clear outer covering of the eyeball.

cortex the wrinkled outer layer of the brain.

decibel a unit for measuring sound.

dermis the skin's inner layer.

epidermis the outer layer of the skin.

evaporate to change from a liquid form into a gas.

farsighted being able to see distant things clearly, but close things look blurred.

focus the point at which light rays meet to make an image.

hay fever a disease caused by a reaction to pollen from leaves, flowers, and trees.

hearing aid something that makes sounds louder in the ear.

iris the eye's colored part.

lens the transparent, jelly-like window through which light enters the eye.

lip-read   understanding what a person is saying by watching the movements of the lips.

microscope   an instrument that makes small objects look larger.

motor nerve   a nerve that carries messages from the brain to the muscles.

muscle   a type of material in the body that can shorten itself to produce movement.

nasal cavity   the hollow area in the upper part of the nose.

nearsighted   only able to see things close by. Anything farther away is blurred.

nerve   one of the tiny threads that pass messages from all parts of the body to the brain and back again.

ophthalmoscope   an instrument for viewing inside the eye.

optic nerve   the nerve leading from the eye to the brain.

papillae   bumps on the tongue that include groups of cells that sense taste.

pores   tiny holes in the skin. Sweat comes out of pores.

pressure   the amount of force of one thing pushing against another.

pupil   the black hole in the center of the eye.

retina   a layer at the back of the eye, sensitive to light.

rods   cells at the back of the eye. They can see in dim light but can only make out black and white.

sclera   the white part of the eye around the iris.

semicircular canals   three tubes in the inner ear that control balance.

senses   parts all over the body that take in information about the outside world and pass messages to the brain.

sensory deprivation   when one or all the senses is cut off.

sensory nerves   nerves that take messages from the senses to the brain.

sensory receptor   the nerve cells at the end of the sensory nerves that receive signals and pass them to the brain.

speech therapist   someone who is trained to help people who have speech problems.

sweat   water containing some of the body's wastes that passes out of the body through the skin.

taste bud   parts on the tongue with sensors to taste food.

vibrate   to move very quickly to and fro or to shake.

voluntary   something that does not happen automatically, but is controlled by thought.

Index

© Heinemann Children's Reference 1990
Artwork © BLA Publishing Limited 1987

Material used in this book first appeared in
Macmillan World Library: HOW OUR BODIES WORK: *The Five Senses.*

Photographic credits
(*t* = top *b* = bottom *l* = left *r* = right)
cover: © James Minor
4*t* Sporting Pictures; 4*b* Science Photo Library; 5 Mountain Camera; 6 The Hutchison Library; 7*t* Vivien Fifield; 7*b* Mary Evans Picture Library; 8 Science Photo Library; 9 Rex Features; 11, 13*t*, 13*b*, 14 Trevor Hill; 15*t* J. Allan Cash; 15*b* Trevor Hill; 16 Science Photo Library; 17, 19*t*, 19*b*, 21*t*, 21*b* Trevor Hill; 23*t*, 23*b* J. Allan Cash; 24 ZEFA; 25, 26 Trevor Hill; 27*t*, 27*b* Science Photo Library; 29*t*, 29*b*, 31*t*; 31*b*, 32 Trevor Hill; 33*t* J. Allan Cash; 33, 34*t*, 34*b*, 35 Trevor Hill; 36 The Guide Dogs for the Blind Association; 37*t*, 37*b* Science Photo Library; 38 Trevor Hill; 39*t* Twinings; 39*b* J. Allan Cash; 40 ZEFA; 41*t* Chris Fairclough Picture Library; 41*b* Mountain Camera; 43 Trevor Hill; 44 Frank Lane Picture Library; 45*t*, 45*b* Science Photo Library